Are You A Bromide?

Gelett Burgess

Table of Contents

Are You A Bromide?

Gelett Burgess

Kessinger Publishing reprints thousands of hard–to–find books!

Visit us at http://www.kessinger.net

```
Are You A Bromide?
      The Sulphitic Theory Expounded And Exemplified According
      To The Most Recent Researches Into The Psychology Of Boredom
      Including Many Well-Known Bromidioms Now In Use
```

Are You A Bromide?

ARE YOU A BROMIDE?

OR,

THE SULPHITIC THEORY

EXPOUNDED AND EXEMPLIFIED ACCORDING TO THE MOST RECENT RESEARCHES INTO THE PSYCHOLOGY OF BOREDOM

Including many well−known Bromidioms now in use

BY

GELETT BURGESS, S.B.

Author of "Goops and How to Be Them," "The Burgess Nonsense Book," "Vivette," &c., &c.

WITH DECORATIONS BY THE AUTHOR

Note: Decorations replaced with five asterisks
  * * * * *

1906

NOTE

 This essay is reprinted, with revisions and enlargement additions, from "The Sulphitic Theory" published in "The Smart Set" for April, 1906, by consent of the editors.

TO

GERTRUDE McCALL

CHATELAINE OF MAC MANOR

Are You A Bromide?

[Illustration]

AND DISCOVERER OF

THE SULPHITIC THEORY

ARE YOU A BROMIDE?

The terms "Bromide" and "Sulphite" as applied to psychological rather than chemical analysis have already become, among the *illuminati*, so widely adopted that these denominations now stand in considerable danger of being weakened in significance through a too careless use. The adjective "bromidic" is at present adopted as a general vehicle, a common carrier for the thoughtless damnation of the Philistine. The time has come to formulate, authoritatively, the precise scope of intellect which such distinctions suggest and to define the shorthand of conversation which their use has made practicable. The rapid spread of the theory, traveling from Sulphite to Sulphite, like the spark of a pyrotechnic set−piece, till the thinking world has been over−violently illuminated, has obscured its genesis and diverted attention from the simplicity and force of its fundamental principles.[1] In this, its progress has been like that of slang, which, gaining in popularity, must inevitably decrease in aptness and definiteness.

[Footnote 1: It was in April that I first heard of the Theory from the Chatelaine. The following August, in Venice, a lady said to me: "Aren't these old palaces a great deal more sulphitic in their decay than they were originally, during the Renaissance?"]

In attempting to solve the problem which for so long was the despair of philosophers I have made modest use of the word "theory." But to the Sulphite, this simple, convincing, comprehensive explanation is more; it is an opinion, even a belief, if not a *credo*. It is the *crux* by which society is tested. But as I shall proceed scientifically, my conclusion will, I trust, effect rational proof of what was an *a priori* hypothesis.

* * * * *

The history of the origin of the theory is brief. The Chatelaine of a certain sugar plantation in Louisiana, in preparing a list of guests for her house−party, discovered, in one of those explosive moments of inspiration, that all people were easily divided into two fundamental groups or families, the Sulphites and the Bromides. The revelation was apodictic, convincing; it made life a different thing; it made society almost plausible. So, too, it simplified human relationship and gave the first hint of a method by which to adjust and equalize affinities. The primary theorems sprang quickly into her mind, and, such is their power, they have attained almost the nature of axioms. The discovery, indeed, was greater, more far−reaching than she knew, for, having undergone the test of philosophical analysis as well as of practical application, it stands, now, a vital, convincing interpretation of the mysteries of human nature.

* * * * *

We have all tried our hands at categories. Philosophy is, itself, but a system of definitions. What, then, made the Chatelaine's theory remarkable, when Civilization has wearied itself with distinctions? The attempt to classify one's acquaintance is the common sport of the thinker, from the fastidious who says: "There are two kinds of persons—those who like olives and those who don't," to the fatuous, immemorial lover who says: "There are two kinds of women—Daisy, and the Other Kind!"

* * * * *

Previous attempts, less fantastic, have had this fault in common: their categories were susceptible of gradation—extremes fused one into the other. What thinking person has not felt the need of some definite, final, absolute classification? We speak of "my kind" and "the other sort," of Those who Understand, of Impossibles, and Outsiders. Some of these categories have attained considerable vogue. There is the Bohemian versus the Philistine, the Radical versus the Conservative, the Interesting versus the Bores, and so on. But always there is a shifting population at the vague frontier—the types intermingle and lose identity. Your Philistine is the very one who says: "This is Liberty Hall!"—and one must drink beer whether one likes it or not. It is the conservative business man, hard−headed, stubborn, who is converted by the mind−reader or the spiritualistic medium—one extreme flying to the other. It is the bore who, at times, unconsciously to himself, amuses you to the point of repressed laughter. These terms are fluent—your friends have a way of escaping from the labeled boxes into which you have put them; they seem to defy your definitions, your Orders and Genera. Fifteen minutes' consideration of the great Sulphitic Theory will, as the patent medicines say, convince one of its efficacy. A Bromide will never jump out of his box into that ticketed

Are You A Bromide?

"Sulphite."

* * * * *

So much comment has been made upon the terminology of this theory that it should be stated frankly, at the start, that the words Sulphite and Bromide, and their derivatives, sulphitic and bromidic, are themselves so sulphitic that they are not susceptible of explanation. In a word, they are empirical, although, accidentally it might seem, they do appeal and convince the most skeptical. I myself balked, at first, at these inconsequent names. I would have suggested the terms "Gothic" and "Classic" to describe the fundamental types of mind. But it took but a short conversation with the Chatelaine to demonstrate the fact that the words were inevitable, and the rapid increase in their use has proved them something more real than slang—an acceptable and accepted terminology. Swallow them whole, therefore, and you will be so much better for the dose that, upon finishing this thesis you will say, "Why, *of course* there are no other words possible!"

Let us, therefore, first proceed with a general statement of the theory and then develop some of its corollaries. It is comparatively easy to define the Bromide; let us consider his traits and then classify the Sulphite by a mere process of exclusion.

* * * * *

In this our world the Bromides constitute, alas! by far the larger group. In this, the type resembles the primary bodies or other systems of classification, such as the Philistines, the Conservatives, the Bores and so on, *ad nauseam*. The Bromide does his thinking by syndicate. He follows the main traveled roads, he goes with the crowd. In a word, they all think and talk alike—one may predicate their opinion upon any given subject. They follow custom and costume, they obey the Law of Averages. They are, intellectually, all peas in the same conventional pod, unenlightened, prosaic, living by rule and rote. They have their hair cut every month and their minds keep regular office hours. Their habits of thought are all ready–made, proper, sober, befitting the Average Man. They worship dogma. The Bromide conforms to everything sanctioned by the majority, and may be depended upon to be trite, banal and arbitrary.

So much has a mere name already done for us that we may say, boldly, and this is our First Theorem: that all Bromides are bromidic in every manifestation of their being. But a

6

better comprehension of the term, and one which will perhaps remove the taint of malediction, will be attained if we examine in detail a few essential bromidic tendencies. The adjective is used more in pity than in anger or disgust. The Bromide can't possibly help being bromidic—though, on the other hand, he wouldn't if he could.

* * * * *

The chief characteristic, then, seems to be a certain reflex psychological action of the bromidic brain. This is evidenced by the accepted bromidic belief that each of the ordinary acts of life is, and necessarily must be, accompanied by its own especial remark or opinion. It is an association of ideas intensified in each generation by the continual correlation of certain groups of brain cells. It has become not only unnecessary for him to think, but almost impossible, so deeply these well—worn paths of thought have become. His intellectual processes are automatic—his train of thought can never get off the track.

* * * * *

A single illustration will suffice for analysis. You have heard it often enough; fie upon you if you have said it!

"If you saw that sunset painted in a picture, you'd never believe it would be possible!"

* * * * *

It must be borne distinctly in mind that *it is not merely because this remark is trite that it is bromidic*; it is because that, with the Bromide, the remark is *inevitable*. One expects it from him, and one is never disappointed. And, moreover, it is always offered by the Bromide as a fresh, new, apt and rather clever thing to say. He really believes, no doubt, that it is original—it is, at any rate, neat, as he indicates by his evident expectation of applause. The remark follows upon the physical or mental stimulus as the night the day; he cannot, then, be true to any other impulse. Originality was inhibited in him since his great—grandmother's time. He has "got the habit."

Accepting his irresponsibility, and with all charity to his undeveloped personality, we may note a few other examples of his mental reflexes. The list is long, but it would take a large encyclopaedia to exhaust the subject. The pastime, recently come into vogue, of

7

collecting Bromidioms,[1] is a pursuit by itself, worthy enough of practice if one appreciates the subtleties of the game and does not merely collate hackneyed phrases, irrespective of their true bromidic quality. For our purpose in elucidating the thesis in hand, however, we need cull but a few specimens, leaving the list to be completed by the reader at his leisure.

[Footnote 1: For this apt and cleverly coined word I am indebted to Mr. Frank O'Malley of the New York "Sun," who has been one of the most ardent and discriminating collectors of Bromidioms.]

    * * * * *

If you both happen to know Mr. Smith of Des Moines, the Bromide inevitably will say:

"This world is such a small place, after all, isn't it?"

The Bromide never mentions such a vulgar thing as a birth, but

"The Year Baby Came."

The Bromide's euphemisms are the slang of her caste. When she departs from her visit, she says:

"I've had a perfectly charming time."

"It's SO good of you to have asked me!"

"Now, DO come and see us!"

And when her caller leaves, her mind springs with a snap to fasten the time−worn farewell:

"Now you have found the way, do come often!"

And this piece of ancient cynicism has run through a thousand changes:

Are You A Bromide?

"Of course if you leave your umbrella at home it's sure to rain! "

But comment, to the Sulphite, is unnecessary. These remarks would all be in his Index Epurgatorius, if one were necessary. Except in jest it would never even occur to him to use any of the following remarks:

* * * * *

I.

"I don't know much about Art, but I know what I like."

II.

"My mother is seventy years old, but she doesn't look a day over fifty."

III.

"That dog understands every word I say."

IV.

"You'll feel differently about these things when you're married! "

V.

"It isn't money, it's the PRINCIPLE of the thing I object to. "

VI.

"Why aren't there any good stories in the magazines, nowadays? "

VII.

"I'm afraid I'm not educated up to Japanese prints."

VIII.

"The Japanese are such an interesting little people!"

IX.

"No, I don't play chess. I haven't got that kind of a brain."

X.

"No, I never intend to be married."

XI.

"I thought I loved him at the time, but of course it wasn't really love."

XII.

"Funny how some people can never learn to spell!"

XIII.

"If you'd only come yesterday, this room was in perfect order."

XIV.

"I don't care for money—it's what I can do with it."

XV.

"I really oughtn't to tell this, but I know you understand."

XVI.

"Why, I know you better than you know yourself!"

XVII.

"Now, this thing really happened!"

XVIII.

"It's a great compliment to have a child fond of you."

XIX.

"The Salvation Army reaches a class of people that churches never do."

XX.

"It's bad enough to see a man drunk—but, oh! a woman!"

XXI.

"It's a mistake for a woman to marry a man younger than herself—women age so much faster than men. Think what she'll be, when he's fifty!"

XXII.

"Of course if you happen to want a policeman, there's never one within miles of you."

XXIII.

"It isn't so much the heat (or the cold), as the humidity in the air."

XXIV.

"This tipping system is terrible, but what can one do about it? "

XXV.

"I don't know what we ever did without the telephone!"

Are You A Bromide?

XXVI.

"After I've shampooed my hair I can't do a thing with it!"

XXVII.

"I never read serials."

XXVIII.

"No, let me pay! I've got to change this bill anyway."

XXIX.

"You're a sight for sore eyes!"

XXX.

"Come up and see us any time. You'll have to take pot−luck, but you're always welcome."

XXXI.

"There are as many chances to get rich in real estate as there ever were—if you only knew where to find them."

XXXII.

"I'd rather have a good horse than all the automobiles made."

XXXIII.

"The price of autos is bound to come down sooner or later, and then you won't see horses except in menageries."

XXXIV.

Are You A Bromide?

"I'd rather go to a dentist than have my photograph taken."

XXXV.

"Did you ever know of a famous man's son who amounted to anything?"

XXXVI.

"The most ignorant Italian laborer seems to be able to appreciate art."

XXXVII.

"I want to see my own country before I go abroad."

XXXVIII.

"Yes, but you can live in Europe for half what you can at home."

XXXIX.

"You can live twenty years in New York and never know who your next door neighbor is."

XL.

"No, I'd just as lief stand; I've been sitting down all day."

XLI.

"Funny how people always confide their love−affairs to me!"

XLII.

"I'd rather be blind than deaf—it's such a tax on your friends."

XLIII.

Are You A Bromide?

"I haven't played a game of billiards for two years, but I'll try, just for the fun of it."

XLIV.

"If you could only write stories the way you tell them, you'd make your fortune as an author."

XLV.

"Nothing can stop a cold, unless you take it right at the start."

XLVI.

"He's told that lie so often that he believes it himself, now."

XLVII.

"If you stay here a year you'll never want to go back."

XLVIII.

"Don't worry; that won't help matters any."

* * * * *

Sulphites are agreed upon most of the basic facts of life, and this common understanding makes it possible for them to eliminate the obvious from their conversation. They have found, for instance, that green is restful to the eyes, and the fact goes without saying, in a hint, in a mere word. They are aware that heat is more disagreeable when accompanied by a high degree of humidity, and do not put forth this axiom as a sensational discovery. They have noticed the coincidences known as mental telepathy usual in correspondence, and have long ceased to be more than mildly amused at the occurrence of the phenomenon. They do not speak in awe-struck voices of supernatural apparitions, for of all fiction the ghost story is most apt to be bromidic, nor do they expect others to be impressed by their strange dreams any more than with their pathological symptoms. Hypnotism, they are convinced, has attained the standing of a science whose rationale is

14

pretty well understood and established, and the subject is no longer an affording subject for anecdote. Sulphites can even listen to tales of Oriental magic, miraculously–growing trees, disappearing boys and what–not, without suggesting that the audience was mesmerized. Above all, the Sulphite recognizes as a principle that, if a story is really funny, it is probably untrue, and he does not seek to give an adjuvant relish to it, by dilating with verisimilitude upon the authenticity of the facts in the case. But your Bromide is impressive and asserts, "I knew the man that died!" The Sulphite, too, has little need for euphemisms. He can speak of birth and death without metaphor.

But to the Bromide all such matters of fact and fancy are perpetually picturesque, and, a discoverer, he leaps up and shouts out enthusiastically that two and two are four, and defends his statement with eloquent logic. Each scene, each incident has its magic spell—like the little woolly toy lamb, he presses the fact, and " ba—ba" the appropriate sentiment comes forth. Does he have, back in the shadows of his mind, perhaps, the ghost of a perception that the thing has been said before? Who can tell! But, if he does, his vanity exorcises the spirit. Bromides seldom listen to one another; they are content with talk for talk's sake, and so escape all chance of education. It is this fact, most likely, which has endowed the bromidiom with immortality. Never heard, it seems always new, appropriate, clever.

No, it Isn't so much the things they say, as the way they say them! Do you not recall the smug, confident look, the assurance of having said a particularly happy thing? They come inevitably as the alarm clock; when the hands of circumstance touch the hour, the bromidic remark will surely go off.

* * * * *

But, lest one make too much of this particular symptom, let us consider a few other tendencies. The Bromide has no surprises for you. When you see one enter a room, you must reconcile yourself to the inevitable. No hope for flashes of original thought, no illuminating, newer point of view, no sulphitic flashes of fancy—the steady glow of bromidic conversation and action is all one can hope for. He may be wise and good, he may be loved and respected—but he lives inland; he puts not forth to sea. He is there when you want him, always the same.

Bromides also enjoy pathological symptoms. They are fond of describing sickness and death–bed scenes. "His face swelled up to twice its natural size!" they say, in awed whispers. They attend funerals with interest and scrutiny.

* * * * *

We are all born with certain bromidic tendencies, and children are the greatest bromides in the world. What boy of ten will wear a collar different from what his school–mates are all wearing? He must conform to the rule and custom of the majority or he suffers fearfully. But, if he has a sulphitic leaven in his soul, adolescence frees him from the tyrannical traditions of thought. In costume, perhaps, men still are more bromidic than women. A man has, for choice, a narrow range in garments—for everyday wear at most but four coats, three collars and two pairs of shoes.

Fewer women become Sulphites. The confession is ungallant and painful, but it must be made. We have only to watch them, to listen—and to pity.

But stay! If there is anything in heredity, women should be most sulphitic. For of all Bromides Adam was the progenitor, while Eve was a Sulphite from the first!

Alice in Wonderland, however, is the modern type—a Bromide amidst Sulphites.

* * * * *

What, then, is a Sulphite? Ah, that is harder to define. A Sulphite is a person who does his own thinking, he is a person who has surprises up his sleeve. He is explosive. One can never foresee what he will do, except that it will be a direct and spontaneous manifestation of his own personality.

You cannot tell them by the looks. Sulphites come together like drops of mercury, in this bromidic world. Unknown, unsuspected groups of them are scattered over the earth, and we never know where we are going to meet them—like fireflies in Summer, like Americans in Europe. The Bromide we have always with us, predicating the obvious. The Sulphite appears uncalled.

* * * * *

Are You A Bromide?

But you must not jump to the conclusion that all Sulphites are agreeable company. This is no classification as of desirable and undesirable people. The Sulphite, from his very nature, must continually surprise you by an unexpected course of action. He must explode. You never know what he will say or do. He is always sulphitic, but as often impossible. He will not bore you, but he may shock you. You find yourself watching him to see what is coming next, and it may be a subtle jest, a paradox, or an atrocious violation of etiquette.

* * * * *

All cranks, all reformers, and most artists are sulphitic. The insane asylums are full of Sulphites. They not only do ordinary things in unusual ways, but they do unusual things in ordinary ways. What is more intensely sulphitic than, when you have said your farewells, to go immediately? Or, as you swim out to rescue a drowning girl, to keep your pipe burning, all the while? They do not attempt to "entertain" you, but let you choose your own pastime. When they present a gift, it has either rhyme or reason to it. Their letters are not passed about to be read by the family.

* * * * *

Hamlet was a Sulphite; Polonius a Bromide. Becky Sharp was sulphitic; Amelia Sedley bromidic. So we might follow the line of cleavage between the two groups in Art, Religion and Politics. Compare, for instance, President Roosevelt with his predecessor in office—the Unexpected versus the sedate Thermometer of Public Opinion. Compare Bernard Shaw with Marie Corelli—one would swear that their very brains were differently colored! Their epigrams and platitudes are merely the symptoms of different methods of thought. One need not consult one's prejudice, affection or taste—the Sulphitic Theory explains without either condemning or approving. The leopard cannot change his spots.

* * * * *

But if, along with these contrasts, we take, for example, Lewis Carroll as opposed to Dr. Johnson, we are brought up against an extraordinary inconsistency. It is, however, only an apparent paradox—beneath it lies a vital principle. Dr. Johnson was, himself, a Sulphite of the Sulphites, but how intensely bromidic were his writings! One yawns to

17

think of them. As for Lewis Carroll, in his classic nonsense, so sulphitic as often to be accused by Bromides of having a secret meaning, his private life was that of a Bromide. Read his biography and learn the terrors of his formal, set entertainments to the little girls whom he patronized! They knew what to expect of him, and he never, however agreeably, disappointed them. No, unfortunately a Sulphite does not always produce sulphitic art. How many writers we know who are more interesting than their work! How many who are infinitely less so! Your professional humorist is usually a dull, melancholy fellow in his private life—and a clergyman may preach infant damnation and be a merry father at home.

* * * * *

Such considerations point inevitably to the truth that our theory depends essentially not upon action or talk, but upon the quality and rationale of thought. It is a question of Potentiality, rather than of Dynamics. It is the process of reasoning which concerns us, not its translation into conduct. A man may be a devoted supporter of Mrs. Grundy and yet be a Sulphite, if he has, in his own mind, reached an original conclusion that society needs her safeguards. He may be the wildest–eyed of Anarchists and yet bromidic, if he has accepted another's reasons and swallowed the propaganda whole.

It will be doubtless through a misconception of this principle that the first schism in the Sulphitic Theory arises. Already the cult has become so important that a newer heretic sect threatens it. These protestants cannot believe that there is a definite line to be drawn between Sulphites and Bromides, and hold that one may partake of a dual nature. All such logic is fatuous, and founded upon a misconception of the Theory.

* * * * *

There is, however, a subtlety which has perhaps had something to do with confusing the neophyte. It is this: Sulphitism and Bromidism are, symbolically, the two halves of a circle, and their extremes meet. One may be so extremely bromidic that one becomes, at a leap, sulphitic, and *vice versa*. This may be easily illustrated.

* * * * *

18

Are You A Bromide?

Miss Herford's inimitable monologues, being each the apotheosis of some typical Bromide—a shopgirl, a country dressmaker, a bargain-hunter and so on—become, through her art, intensely sulphitic. They are excruciatingly funny, just because she represents types so common that we recognize them instantly. Each expresses the crystallized thought of her particular bromidic group. Done, then, by a person who is herself a Sulphite *par excellence*, the result is droll. "One has," says Emerson, "but to remove an object from its environment and instantly it becomes comic."

* * * * *

The same thing is done less artistically every day upon the vaudeville stage. We love to recognize types; and what Browning said of beauty:

We're made so that we love
First, when we see them painted,
Things we have passed
Perhaps a hundred times nor cared to see

can be easily extended to our sense of humor in caricature. A recent hit upon the variety stage does still more to illustrate the problem.

The "Cherry Sisters" aroused immense curiosity by an act so bromidic as to be ridiculous. Were they rank amateurs, doing their simple best, or were they clever artists, simulating the awkward crudeness of country girls? That was the question. In a word, were they Sulphites or Bromides?

What such artists have done histrionically, Hillaire Belloc has done exquisitely for literature in his "Story of Manuel Burden." This tale, affecting to be a serious encomium upon a middle class British merchant, shows plainly that all satire is, in its essence, a sulphitic juggling with bromidic topics. It is done unconsciously by many a simple rhymester whose verses are bought by Sulphites and read with glee.

* * * * *

In the terminology of our theory we must, therefore, include two new terms, describing the variation of intensity of these two different states of mind. The extremes meet at the points of Nitro–Bromidism and Hypo–Sulphitism, respectively. Intensity of Bromidism becomes, then, Nitro–Bromidism, and we have seen how, through the artist's, or through a Sulphite's subtle point of view, such Nitro–Bromide becomes immediately sulphitic.

By a similar reasoning, a Hypo–Sulphite can, at a step, become bromidic. The illustration most obvious is that of insanity. We are not much amused, usually, by the quaint modes of thought exhibited by lunatics and madmen.

It cannot be denied, however, that their processes of thought are sulphitic; indeed, they are so wildly original, so fanciful, that we must denominate all such crazed brains, Hypo–Sulphites. Such persons are so surprising that they end by having no surprises left for us. We accept their mania and cease to regard it; it, in a word, becomes bromidic. So, in their ways, are all cranks and eccentrics, all whose set purpose is to astonish or to shock. We end by being bored at their attitudes and poses.

* * * * *

The Sulphite has the true Gothic spirit; the Bromide, the impulse of the classic. One wonders, relishing the impossible, manifesting himself in characteristic, spontaneous ways; the other delights in rule and rhythm, in ordered sequences, in authority and precedent, following the law. One carves the gargoyle and ogrillion, working in paths untrod, the other limits himself to harmonic ratios, balanced compositions, and to predestined fenestration. One has a grim, *naif*, virile humor, the other a dead, even beauty. One is hot, the other cold. The Dark Ages were sulphitic—there were wild deeds then; men exploded. The Renaissance was essentially bromidic; Art danced in fetters, men looked back at the Past for inspiration and chewed the cud of Greek thought. For the Sulphite, fancy; for the Bromide, imagination.

* * * * *

From the fifteenth century on, however, the wave of Sulphitism rose steadily, gradually dropping at times into little depressions of Euphuistic manners and intervals of "sensibility" but climbing, with the advance of science and the emancipation of thought to an ideal—the personal, original interpretation of life. The nineteenth century showed curiously erratic variations of the curve. From its beginning till 1815, Sulphitism was upon the increase, while from that year till 1870 there was a sickening drop to the veriest depths of bromidic thought. Then the Bromide infested the earth. With his black–walnut furniture, his jig–saw and turning–lathe methods of decoration, his lincrusta–walton and pressed terracotta, his chromos, wax flowers, hoop skirts, chokers, side whiskers and pantalettes, went a horrific revival of mock modesty inspired by the dying efforts of the old formulated religious thought. And then——when steam had had its day, impressing its materialism upon the world; making what should be hard, easy, and what should be easy, hard—came electricity—a new science almost approaching a spiritual force, and, with a rush, the telephone that made the commonplace bristle with romance! The curve of sulphitism arose. A wave of Oriental thought lifted many to a curious idealism—and, as so many other centuries had done before, there came to the nineteenth a *fin de siecle* glow that lifted up the curve still higher. The Renaissance of thought came—came the cult of simplicity and Mission furniture—corsets were abandoned—the automobile freed us from the earth—the Yellow Book began, Mrs. Eddy appeared, radium was discovered and appendicitis flourished.

* * * * *

So there are bromidic vegetables like cabbage, and sulphitic ones like garlic. The distinction, once understood, applies to almost everything thinkable. There are bromidic titles to books and stories, and titles sulphitic. "The Something of Somebody" is, at present, the commonest bromidic form. Once, as in "The Courting of Dinah Shadd" and "The Damnation of Theron Ware," such a title was sulphitic, but one cannot pick up a magazine, nowayears, without coming across "The ——of ——" As most magazines are edited for Middle Western Bromides, such titles are inevitable. I know of one, with a million circulation, which accepted a story with the sulphitic title, "Thin Ice," and changed it to the bromidic words, "Because Other Girls were Free." One of O. Henry's first successful stories, and perhaps his best humorous tale, had its title so changed from "Cupid *a la carte*," to "A Guthrie Wooing."

This is one of the few exceptions to the rule that a sulphitic thing can become bromidic. Time alone can accomplish this effect. Literature itself is either bromidic or sulphitic. The dime novel and melodrama, with hackneyed situations, once provocative, are so easily nitro–bromidic that they become sulphitic in burlesque and parody.

* * * * *

Are You A Bromide?

Metaphysically, Sulphitism is easily explained by the theory of Absolute Age. We have all seen children who seem to be, mentally, with greater possibility of growth than their parents. We see persons who understand without experience. It is as if they had lived before. It is as if they had a definite Absolute Age. We recognize and feel sympathetic with those of our caste—with those of the same age, not in years, but in wisdom. Now the standard of spiritual insight is the person of a thousand years of age. He knows the relative Importance of Things. And it might be said, then, that Bromides are individuals of less than five hundred years; Sulphites, those who are over that age. In some dim future incarnation, perhaps, the Bromide will leap into sulphitic apprehension of existence. It is the person who is Absolutely Young who says, "Alas, I never had a youth—I don't understand what it is to be young!" and he who is Absolutely Old remarks, blithely, "Oh, dear, I can't seem to grow up at all!" One is a Bromide and the other a Sulphite—and this explanation illuminates the paradox.

* * * * *

The Sulphite brings a fresh eye to life. He sees everything as if for the first time, and not through the blue glasses of convention. As if he were a Martian newly come to earth, he sees things separated from their environment, tradition, precedent—the dowager without her money, the politician without his power, the sage without his poverty; he sees men and women for himself. He prefers his own observation to any *a priori* theories of society. He knows how to work, but he knows, too (what the Bromide does never), how to play, and he plays with men and women for the joy of life, and his own particular game. Though his view he eccentric it is his own view, and though you may avoid him, you can never forget or ignore him.

* * * * *

And so, too, using an optical symbolism, we may speak of the Sulphite as being refractive—every impression made upon him is split up into component rays of thought—he sees beauty, humor, pathos, horror, and sublimity. The Bromide is reflective, and the object is thrown back unchanged, unanalyzed; it is accepted without interrogation. The mirrored bromidic mind gives back only what it has taken. To use the phraseology of Harvard and Radcliffe, the Sulphite is connotative, the Bromide denotative.

Are You A Bromide?

* * * * *

But the theory is constructive rather than destructive. It makes for content, and peace. By this philosophy one sees one's friends revealed. Though the Bromide will never say whether he prefers dark or white meat; though he inflict upon you the words, "Why, if two hundred years ago people had been told that you could talk through a wire they would have hanged the prophet for witchcraft!" though he repeats the point of his story, rolling it over on his tongue, seeking for a second laugh; though he says, "Dinner is my best meal"—he cannot help it. You know he is a Bromide, and you expect no more.

* * * * *

You will notice, also, in discussing this theory with your friends, that the Bromide will take up, with interest, only the bromidic aspect of life. The term will amuse him, and, never thinking that it should be applied to himself, he will use the word "Bromide" in season and out of it. To the Sulphite, however, Sulphitism is a thing to be watched for, cultivated, and treasured. He will search long for the needle in the haystack, and leave the bromidiom to be observed by the careless, thoughtless Bromide. And, as the supreme test, it may be remarked that, should buttons be put on the market, bearing the names "Bromide" and "Sulphite" in blue and red, a few minutes' reflection will convince the Sulphite that, before long, all the Bromides would be wearing the red Sulphite buttons, and all the Sulphites the blue Bromide. Such is the rationale of the perverse.

* * * * *

Bromides we may love, and even marry. Your own mother, your sister, your sweetheart, may be bromidic, but you are not less affectionate. They are restful and soporific. You may not have understood them; before you heard of the Sulphitic Theory you were annoyed at their dullness, their dogmas, but, with this white light illuminating them, you accept them, now, for what they are, and, expecting nothing original from them, you find a new peace and a new joy in their society. "You may estimate your capacity for the Comic," says Meredith—and the statement might be applied as well to the Bromidic—"by being able to detect the ridicule of them you love, without loving them less."

* * * * *

23

Are You A Bromide?

The Bromide has no salt nor spice nor savor—but he is the bread of Society, the veriest staff of life. And if, like Little Jack Horner, you can occasionally put in your thumb and pull out a sulphitic plum from your acquaintance, be thankful for that, too!

CPSIA information can be obtained
at www.ICGtesting.com
Printed in the USA
BVHW061351260721
612866BV00013B/708